A I S L E S *of*
ADVENTURE ™

Discover Strawberries

Helen A. Kudzin

STRAWBERRIES

by Helen A. Kudzin

First Printing – April 2004

Copyright © Aisles of Adventure™, a Division of HAK Publishing Inc. 2004

"™– Trademark of HAK Publishing Inc."

HAK Publishing Inc.
#300, 8120 Beddington Blvd., NW
Calgary, Alberta, Canada T3K 2A8

National Library of Canada Cataloguing in Publication

Kudzin, Helen A.

Discover strawberries : aisles of adventure™ / Helen A. Kudzin; edited by Margo Embury; photographer Patricia Holdsworth.

Includes index.
ISBN 1-897010-01-X (pbk.)

1. Cookery (Strawberries) I. Embury, Margo, 1943- II. Title.

TX813.S9K84 2004	641.6'475	C2004-902186-9

Photography by Patricia Holdsworth, Patricia Holdsworth Photography

Page design by Brian Danchuk, Brian Danchuk Design

Page formatting by Iona Glabus

Designed, Printed and Produced in Canada by:
Centax Books, a Division of PrintWest Communications Ltd.
Publishing Director, Photo Designer and Food Stylist: Margo Embury
1150 Eighth Avenue, Regina, Saskatchewan, Canada S4R 1C9
(306) 525-2304   FAX (306) 757-2439
E-mail: centax@printwest.com   www.centaxbooks.com

TABLE OF CONTENTS

Note: All recipes have been tested using large eggs. All recipes have been tested using standard measurements. While metric conversions have been provided as a convenience, the recipes have not been tested in metric.

STRAWBERRY HISTORY & NOTES

Strawberries have a long history, but it is difficult to trace both in terms of ancestry and name. The French, Spanish and Italians referred to the fruit as "fraise" or fragrant berry, the North American Narraganset Indians as "wuttahimneash" or heart berry, and the English as "strawberry" which is thought to have several possible origins. The runners which the plants prolifically produce were said to be "strewn" around the plants – some early literature refers to the fruit as "strewberries." A second theory is that straw was used as mulch around the plants during the winter months, used as a weed control during the growing season, and to keep the berries cleaner for harvest – therefore, the reference to straw. In London, children used to gather the berries in the woodlands and string them on pieces of straw for sale in the markets – hence "straws of berries." Over time, many modifications appeared, including straberry, streberie, straibery, straubery and finally "strawberry."

The wild strawberry plant is indigenous to both the northern and southern hemispheres and was found growing in woodlands, mountainous areas and along the seaside. Strawberries date back 2,200 years, to ancient Rome, with some of the earliest accounts appearing in the writings of Cato, a Roman Senator circa 200 BC. They were also described in literature in 1000 AD; the first botanical drawing of the plant was printed in 1484; and early writings describe the medicinal uses of the plant's leaves and roots versus the benefits of the fruit. Ancient references are difficult to find because they were never cultivated as an agricultural staple until the 1300s and even then they were grown more for their ornamental value. As the consumption of these early strawberries became more widespread in Europe, the plant was transplanted from the woods and propagated by runners, with many people cultivating small patches in their gardens.

Explorers were the first to bring back different types of wild strawberry plants from the new world in the 1500s – Cartier brought plants from Canada to France; Hariot from Virginia to London; the Spanish from Chile and Peru to Spain. The 1500s became important in establishing the botanical knowledge and horticultural significance of the strawberry both as a common garden plant with ornamental value as well as a table delicacy. France became the frontrunner in strawberry cultivation and production and the French King, Louis XIV, chose strawberries as his favorite fruit. But the strawberry as we know it today still had not been developed – not until the mid-1800s did the improvement and breeding of new varieties in Europe and North America finally result in the forerunners to our present big-fruited strawberry.

Today, strawberries are grown in every province and state in Canada and the USA, as well as all over Europe, Australia, Central and South America and the Middle East. They grow on plants very low to the ground, on a stem in groups of three; are propagated by runners that send down roots, not by seeds; change in color as they ripen from a greenish white to a flame red; are very sensitive to small changes in temperature and day length; must be kept weed free during the growing season; and prefer sandier soil and readily available irrigation. Commercially cultivated strawberries require constant attention. The life of a field is not long – only 3 years before replanting is required! Because they are so delicate and perishable, vine-ripened berries are hand-picked daily, sorted and packed in the field, and rushed either to special shipping facilities where they are cooled to about 24°F (-4°C) and loaded on refrigerated trucks within 24 hours, for delivery to consumer markets, or sent to local food processing plants.

STRAWBERRY VARIETIES

The native wild strawberry plants found in North and South America were superior to all the existing European varieties in terms of size, flavor and beauty. In the mid-1700s, Antoine Duchesne, a young French botanist and one of the first and most-noted authorities on the strawberry's classification and history, did much of the early work that led to the development of hybrids which improved the strawberry. But it was the crossing of the North American (Virginia) scarlet variety, that was more adapted to heat, drought and cold, with a hybrid of the South American (Chilean) beach variety, less hardy but yielding large fruit, that was most significant. Without this European interest and effort in strawberry breeding, and the marrying of these two varieties, our modern strawberry would not exist. This variety became known as the Pine Strawberry because of its distinctive flavor. Over the past 250 years, strawberry breeders continued to tackle this biologically complex and sensitive plant, developing many varieties, each with a different commercial focus – size, aroma, flavor, dessert quality, preserving quality, appearance, adaptation to soil conditions, time to maturity, disease resistance, etc.

In North America, the first strawberry hybrid, the "Hudson," was developed in 1780. The next most significant hybrid was the Hoevig, in 1834, followed by many others. Some of our modern varieties include the Hood, Rainer and Totem.

Locally grown strawberries, fresh from the field, are harvested exactly when ready for market – at their sweetest and juiciest, and are meant to be enjoyed quickly. Other commercial and off-season varieties are developed and grown so they are better suited to shipping over long distances and have a longer shelf life. These strawberries are visually stunning but contain more fiber, less sugar and more pectin, making them firmer and good travelers, but at the expense of flavor and juiciness.

NUTRITION

Strawberries aren't just great tasting, they are loaded with good nutrition! Eight medium strawberries have more Vitamin C than an orange – your entire daily requirement. Rich in potassium; folic acid (important for pregnant women and a heart-disease fighter); dietary fiber and antioxidants, there are only 50 calories in those eight strawberries. Doctors and scientists are now discovering that this luscious little berry may also play a role in benefiting our cardiovascular systems by helping to lower the LDL or bad component of cholesterol, and may even be an effective cancer fighter. Pretty impressive health benefits for something that tastes so fabulous!

BELIEVE IT OR NOT

The strawberry is a member of the rose family. Its botanical name is "frugaria," meaning fragrance in Latin. Considered an aphrodisiac in medieval times, it is a symbol for Venus, the Goddess of Love, because of its heart shape and red color. The only fruit that carries its seeds on the outside of its flesh, it is not considered a true berry. If you break a double strawberry in half and share it with a member of the opposite sex, legend has it you will fall in love with each other. There is a strawberry museum in Wepion, Belgium.

SELECTING AND STORING

Look for berries that are plump, bright red and shiny, with fresh green hulls. Berries that have large green or white shoulders are under-ripe, and strawberries do not ripen after picking. Avoid a box with mouldy berries on top – it could be a sign that the quality of the entire box has been compromised. Pick the berries over before storing, removing those that are damaged. They are best stored unwashed, loosely covered with plastic wrap and refrigerated until ready to use. Just before using, gently rinse with cool water, quickly pat dry with a towel and remove the hulls, if you wish.

Generally, strawberries don't keep well. Storage times vary depending on the type of strawberry – those fresh from local fields have a very short life – just a day or two. Other varieties grown for their travel qualities last about a week.

FREEZING

What a great way to capture and preserve an abundance of berries, while they are inexpensive, in season and at the peak of flavor. There is no need to ever do without enjoying this delicious and healthful fruit any time of year. See the freezing information on page 48.

Please enjoy the variety of strawberry recipes presented.

Ready your ingredients. It's time to DISCOVER your favorites!

STRAWBERRY-BANANA SMOOTHIE

A dynamite breakfast in a glass.

Required: *blender*   **Makes**: *2 servings – about 3 cups (750 mL)*

1	cup	vanilla-flavored yogurt	250	mL
1¹/₂	cups	fresh or frozen whole strawberries	375	mL
1		frozen banana, cut up	1	
¹/₄	cup	orange juice	60	mL
2	tbsp.	honey	30	mL

- Place all ingredients in a blender, cover and blend until very smooth.

Variations:

- Omit the orange juice and add ¹/₂ cup (125 mL) milk and ¹/₄ cup (60 mL) peanut butter.
- Try different juices and different flavors of yogurt to suit your taste.

STRAWBERRY LEMONADE

Absolutely refreshing on a hot summer day.

Required: *large pitcher*   **Makes**: *8 servings– about 2 quarts (2 L)*

2	cups	halved fresh strawberries	500	mL
1	cup	freshly squeezed lemon juice	250	mL
¹/₂	cup	granulated sugar, or more to taste	125	mL
3	cups	club soda, chilled	750	mL
		ice		

- Place the strawberries, lemon juice and sugar in a blender, cover and purée until smooth. Pour into a large pitcher.
- Add the club soda **slowly** and stir. Serve over ice.

Variation:

- For **Strawberry Limeade**, use freshly squeezed lime juice instead of the lemon juice.

Pictured on page 17.

STRAWBERRY CHAMPAGNE SPARKLERS
Wonderful for a summer brunch.

Required: blender, large pitcher   **Makes**: 6-8 servings – about 1$^1/_2$ quarts (1.5 L)

2	cups	chopped ripe strawberries	500	mL
2$^1/_2$	cups	cranberry juice	625	mL
26	oz.	champagne, chilled	750	mL

- Place strawberries in a blender – cover and purée until smooth. Measure out 1$^1/_3$ cups (325 mL) of purée.
- Add the cranberry juice and blend until combined. Pour into a large pitcher and refrigerate until ready to use.
- Pour in the champagne and stir to mix. Serve in stemmed glasses.

Variation:
- Use a 10$^1/_2$ oz. (300 g) pkg. frozen whole strawberries instead of fresh.
- Use any chilled, sparkling white or rosé wine instead of champagne.

STRAWBERRY DAIQUIRI
A frozen, thick, slushy daiquiri – perfect!

Required: blender   **Makes**: 4 servings – about 4 cups (1 L)

4	cups	frozen whole strawberries	1	L
$^2/_3$	cup	rum	150	mL
$^1/_2$	cup	freshly squeezed lime juice	125	mL
$^1/_4$	cup	berry sugar	60	mL

- Thaw the strawberries just a tiny bit. Place in a blender along with the rum, lime juice and sugar. Cover and purée until smooth.
- Serve immediately with a straw. Garnish with a fresh strawberry.

Pictured on page 18.

STRAWBERRY CREAM AMARETTO

Smooth and creamy – serve instead of dessert!

Required: *blender*   **Makes:** *2 servings – 1¹/₂ cups (375 mL)*

1¹/₂ oz.	Bailey's Irish cream liqueur	45	mL
1¹/₂ oz.	amaretto liqueur	45	mL
²/₃ cup	frozen sliced strawberries in syrup, partially thawed	150	mL
¹/₂ cup	crushed ice	125	mL
	whole fresh strawberries for garnish		

- Combine the Bailey's, amaretto, strawberries and ice in a blender and purée.
- Pour into stemmed glasses and garnish with a whole strawberry (slice strawberry part way through and place on rim of glass).

Pictured on page 36.

STRAWBERRY PUNCH

Beautiful and refreshing, a summer favorite.

Required: *large punch bowl*   **Makes:** *3 quarts (3 L)*

³/₄	cup	granulated sugar	175	mL
3	cups	water	750	mL
2	cups	unsweetened pineapple juice	500	mL
1¹/₄	cups	freshly squeezed orange juice	300	mL
¹/₄	cup	freshly squeezed lemon juice	60	mL
15	oz.	pkg. frozen sliced strawberries in syrup, thawed	425	g
4	cups	lemon-lime soda	1	L
		ice cubes		

- Combine the sugar and water; stir until dissolved. Pour into the punch bowl.
- Stir in the juices and add the thawed strawberries with syrup.
- Pour in the lemon-lime soda and stir. Add some ice cubes.

Variations:

- Make this ahead, except for the lemon-lime soda, and freeze the entire batch of punch in a plastic bowl. Remove from the freezer about 1 hour prior to using; break up into chunks and pour lemon-lime soda over; stir. It will be slushy and have an entirely different texture.
- For a punch with punch, before adding the soda, add 26 oz. (750 mL) of white or sparkling wine or 2-3 cups (500-750 mL) vodka or white rum.

FRENCH TOAST & STRAWBERRY CREAM SAUCE

A special eye-opener or a wonderful brunch dish.

Prep: 30 minutes   **Cook**: 15 minutes total   **Makes**: 4 servings
Required: large non-stick skillet, oiled

STRAWBERRY CREAM SAUCE:

15	oz.	pkg. frozen sliced strawberries in syrup, thawed	425	g
3/4	cup	sour cream	175	mL
1/2	tsp.	ground cinnamon	2	mL

FRENCH TOAST:

1	cup	half & half (cereal) cream	250	mL
2		eggs	2	
1	tbsp.	granulated sugar	15	mL
2	tsp.	vanilla extract	10	mL
1/4	tsp.	salt	1	mL
1 1/2	cups	cornflake crumbs	375	mL
1	tsp.	ground cinnamon	5	mL
8	slices	stale French bread, sliced 1" (2.5 cm.) thick	8	
3	tbsp.	butter OR vegetable oil	45	mL
		icing (confectioner's) sugar for sprinkling (optional)		
4		strawberries for garnish	4	

- **Sauce:** Combine the strawberries, sour cream and cinnamon in a small saucepan. Set over low heat and heat gently – be careful not to boil. Stir occasionally. Set aside.
- **French Toast:** Combine the cream, eggs, sugar, vanilla and salt in a shallow container and whisk until thoroughly blended.
- Combine the cornflake crumbs and cinnamon in a shallow container.
- Dip the bread slices into the egg mixture and then into the cornflake crumbs, coating each side.
- Heat the butter in a skillet over medium heat; place 1-2 coated bread slices in the skillet. Cook until golden and crisp on both sides. Remove from the pan and sprinkle lightly with icing sugar, if you wish. Add more butter to the pan if required. Repeat until all of the bread is cooked.
- Serve with warm Strawberry Cream Sauce. Garnish with whole strawberries.

Variation:

- Substitute grated orange zest for the ground cinnamon.

STRAWBERRY MUFFINS

A favorite during strawberry season. Serve warm from the oven.

Preheat oven to 400°F (200°C).
Prep: *30 minutes*   **Bake**: *20-22 minutes*   **Makes**: *12 big muffins*
Required: *12-cup muffin pan, greased or paper lined*   ***Freezes well***

STREUSEL TOPPING:

$1/3$	cup	all-purpose flour	75	mL
3	tbsp.	packed brown sugar	45	mL
3	tbsp.	butter	45	mL
$1/2$	tsp.	ground cinnamon	2	mL

MUFFIN BATTER:

$2^1/_2$	cups	all-purpose flour	625	mL
$1/2$	cup	granulated sugar	125	mL
4	tsp.	baking powder	20	mL
$3/4$	tsp.	salt	4	mL
$1^1/_4$	cups	diced fresh strawberries	310	mL
$1^1/_3$	cups	milk	325	mL
$1/3$	cup	vegetable oil	75	mL
2		eggs	2	
$1^1/_2$	tsp.	vanilla extract	7	mL
1	tsp.	grated orange zest	5	mL

■ **Streusel**: Mix all of the streusel ingredients in a small bowl, with your fingers, until coarse crumbs form. Set aside.

■ **Batter**: Combine the flour, sugar, baking **powder** and salt in a large bowl. Stir in the diced strawberries, ensuring all the berries are coated. Set aside.

■ Whisk the milk, oil, eggs, vanilla and orange zest in a separate bowl.

■ Add the milk mixture all at once to the dry ingredients. Stir until just combined and no trace of flour remains. The batter will be lumpy.

■ Fill the muffin pans completely full, then sprinkle the streusel mixture over the muffins, pressing lightly into the batter.

■ **Bake for 20-22 minutes**, or until a cake tester inserted in the middle comes out clean.

Variation:

■ Omit the streusel and sprinkle muffins with sugar. Bake as above.

Pictured on page 17.

■

LEMON STRAWBERRY TEA BREAD

Delicious served slightly warm or sliced thickly and toasted.

Preheat oven to 350°F (180°C).   **Freezes well,** *without the glaze*
Prep: *30 minutes*   **Bake**: *70 -75 minutes*   **Makes**: *12 slices*
Required: *8 x 4 x 2^1/$_2$" (20 x 10 x 7 cm) loaf pan, greased and floured*

2	cups	all-purpose flour	500	mL
1	tsp.	baking soda	5	mL
^{1}/$_4$	tsp.	salt	1	mL
2	cups	chopped fresh strawberries	500	mL
2		eggs	2	
^{1}/$_2$	cup	granulated sugar	125	mL
^{1}/$_2$	cup	butter, melted, cooled slightly	125	mL
^{1}/$_3$	cup	milk	75	mL
1	tbsp.	finely grated lemon zest	15	mL
^{1}/$_2$	tsp.	vanilla extract	2	mL

LEMON GLAZE:

^{1}/$_3$	cup	freshly squeezed lemon juice	75	mL
3	tbsp.	granulated sugar	45	mL

- Combine the flour, baking **soda** and salt in a large bowl. Stir in the chopped strawberries, ensuring all the berries are coated. Set aside.
- Beat the eggs and sugar in a separate bowl, with an electric mixer, until light and lemon colored. Stir in the melted butter, milk, lemon zest and vanilla.
- Stir the egg mixture into the dry ingredients and mix by hand until no traces of flour remain. Do not overmix – the batter will be quite thick.
- Scrape the batter into the prepared loaf pan and **bake for 70-75 minutes**, or until a cake tester inserted in the middle comes out clean.
- Remove from the oven and cool in the pan for about 10 minutes.
- **Glaze:** While the loaf is cooling a bit, combine the lemon juice and sugar in a small saucepan and simmer over medium heat until the mixture boils for 2 minutes. Remove from the heat. With a skewer, poke holes in the top of the warm loaf. Drizzle the hot glaze over the loaf, pouring slowly so it can be absorbed. Cool the loaf a bit more and remove from the pan.

STRAWBERRY COFFEE CAKE

Moist, with great strawberry flavor – delicious with a cup of coffee.

Preheat oven to 375°F (190°C).
Prep: *30 minutes*   **Bake:** *35-40 minutes*   **Makes:** *8 servings*
Required: *8" (20 cm) square pan, greased and floured*   **Freezes well**

PECAN CRUMB TOPPING:

1/2	cup	all-purpose flour	125	mL
1/2	cup	granulated sugar	125	mL
1/4	cup	softened butter	60	mL
1/3	cup	finely chopped pecans	75	mL

CAKE BATTER:

1	cup	all-purpose flour	250	mL
1/2	cup	granulated sugar	125	mL
2	tsp.	baking powder	10	mL
1/2	cup	milk	125	mL
2		eggs	2	
2	tbsp.	butter, melted	30	mL
1	tsp.	vanilla extract	5	mL
1½-2 cups		sliced fresh strawberries	375-500	mL

- **Topping:** Mix the topping ingredients in a small bowl until coarse crumbs form – work in with your fingers if necessary. Set aside.
- **Batter:** Combine the flour, sugar and baking **powder** in a large bowl.
- Beat the milk, eggs, melted butter and vanilla in a separate bowl, with an electric mixer, until combined. Add to the dry ingredients and continue to beat on low speed until well blended.
- Pour the batter into the prepared pan and spread evenly. Arrange the strawberries evenly over the batter; sprinkle the crumb topping evenly over the strawberries
- **Bake for 35-40 minutes,** or until lightly browned on top. Remove and cool slightly on a wire rack
- Serve warm at room temperature.

Variation:

- Add 1 tsp. (5 mL) grated lemon zest to the batter instead of the vanilla.

STRAWBERRY SALSA

Hot and sweet – great with toasted pita triangles, grilled meats or seafood.

Prep: *30 minutes*   **Cool**: *2 hours*   **Makes**: *3 cups (750 mL)*
Required: *medium glass bowl*

1¹/₄	cups	diced fresh strawberries	300	mL
¹/₂	cup	finely diced red onion	125	mL
¹/₂	cup	finely diced red bell pepper	125	mL
¹/₂	cup	finely diced yellow bell pepper	125	mL
¹/₂	cup	finely diced green bell pepper	125	mL
2-3	tbsp.	minced jalapeño pepper	30-45	mL
¹/₄	cup	finely diced fresh cilantro	60	mL
3	tbsp	freshly squeezed orange juice	45	mL
2	tbsp.	freshly squeezed lime juice	30	mL
2	tbsp.	olive oil	30	mL
		salt and pepper to taste (optional)		

- Prepare the strawberries, onion, peppers, jalapeño and cilantro. Place in a glass (non-reactive) bowl and set aside.
- Whisk the orange juice, lime juice and olive oil together in a small bowl and gently stir into the salsa ingredients.
- Cover and refrigerate for at least 2 hours to blend flavors prior to serving (no longer than 4 hours).
- Just before serving, add some salt and pepper, if you wish.

SUMMER STRAWBERRY SOUP

A perfect start to a brunch or a continental breakfast.

Prep: *30 minutes* **Chill**: *2-3 hours.* **Makes**: *4-6 servings*
Required: *blender, medium glass bowl* *4¹/₂ cups (1.2 L)*

4	cups	sliced fresh strawberries OR frozen whole berries, thawed, with juices	1	L
1	cup	dry red wine	250	mL
1	cup	granulated sugar	250	mL
¹/₄	cup	freshly squeezed lemon juice	60	mL
2	tsp.	grated lemon zest	10	mL

- Combine all of the ingredients in a blender; cover and purée until smooth.
- Chill the soup in a covered glass (non-reactive) bowl for several hours.
- Garnish individual servings with sliced strawberries and a mint sprig.

Pictured on page 17.

STRAWBERRY BUTTERMILK SOUP

Slightly tart – another great starter for a special brunch or light luncheon.

Prep: *30 minutes* **Chill**: *2-3 hours.* **Makes**: *4-5 servings*
Required: *blender, medium glass bowl* *5 cups (1.2 L)*

3	cups	sliced fresh strawberries (2 cups/500 mL puréed)	750	mL
3	tbsp.	granulated sugar	45	mL
1	tbsp.	cornstarch	15	mL
2¹/₂	cups	cranberry juice	625	mL
1	tbsp.	red wine vinegar	15	mL
1	cup	buttermilk	250	mL

- Place the strawberries in a blender; cover and purée until smooth. Set aside.
- Combine the sugar and cornstarch in a saucepan. Stir in the cranberry juice and vinegar; cook over medium heat, stirring constantly until it just begins to boil and is clear and slightly thickened.
- Stir in the strawberry purée; cook and stir just until the soup begins to boil. Remove from the heat.
- Strain the hot soup to remove seeds and pulp and place in a glass (non-reactive) bowl. Cool slightly, then refrigerate for 2-3 hours.
- Just before serving, stir in the buttermilk.

STRAWBERRY CRANBERRY SALAD

A great alternative to cranberry sauce – serve with roasted turkey or chicken.

Prep: *40 minutes*   **Chill**: *Required*   **Makes**: *10-12 servings*
Required: *large serving bowl*

2	cups	frozen whole strawberries, thawed and drained, juice reserved	500	mL
2x3	oz.	pkgs. strawberry gelatin	2x85	g
1	cup	boiling water	250	mL
1	cup	diced celery	250	mL
1	cup	chopped walnuts	250	mL
14	oz.	can whole cranberry sauce	398	mL
1	tbsp.	lemon juice	15	mL
1¹/₂	tsp.	ground cinnamon	7	mL
¹/₂	tsp.	ground cloves	2	mL

- Thaw strawberries; drain and reserve juice. Add enough water to juice to measure 1 cup (250 mL). Set aside. Chop the strawberries and set aside.
- Dissolve the gelatin in the boiling water. Stir in the strawberry juice and water. Chill until the consistency of unbeaten egg whites.
- Combine the reserved chopped strawberries, celery, walnuts, cranberry sauce, cinnamon and cloves in a separate bowl. Stir into the thickened gelatin.
- Chill until set.

Variation:
- Omit the cinnamon and cloves for a salad with a less "spicy" flavor.

Strawberry Lemonade, page 7
Summer Strawberry Soup, page 15
Strawberry Onion Salad, page 19
Strawberry Muffins, page 11

STRAWBERRY ONION SALAD

Don't let the onions put you off – this is simple and absolutely delicious!

Prep: *20 minutes*   **Makes**: *4-6 servings*
Required: *6 individual salad plates*

CREAMY POPPY SEED DRESSING:

1/4	cup	mayonnaise	60	mL
1/4	cup	sour cream OR plain yogurt	60	mL
1/4	cup	milk	60	mL
1/4	cup	granulated sugar	60	mL
2	tbsp.	red wine vinegar	30	mL
1 1/2	tbsp.	poppy seeds	22	mL
		red leaf lettuce		
2	cups	sliced, fresh strawberries	500	mL
1 1/2	cups	thinly sliced red onion	625	mL

- **Dressing**: Whisk together the mayonnaise, sour cream, milk, sugar, red wine vinegar and poppy seeds until combined and smooth. Set aside.
- Wash and dry the lettuce. Tear it into bite-sized pieces and divide among the salad plates.
- Wash and dry the strawberries and slice thinly. Sprinkle attractively over the lettuce.
- Divide the onion slices among the salad plates.
- Just before serving, pour the dressing over the salads. Refrigerate any leftover dressing.

Pictured on page 17.

Strawberry Daiquiri, page 8
Spicy Strawberry Spinach Salad, page 20
Strawberry Chicken Stir-Fry, page 24

SPICY STRAWBERRY SPINACH SALAD

This spicy dressing will leave you begging for more.

Prep: 20 minutes   **Makes**: 4-6 servings
Required: large serving bowl

1¹/₂	cups	sliced fresh strawberries	375	mL
1	bunch	fresh spinach, washed and dried	1	

SPICY RED WINE DRESSING:

¹/₄	cup	vegetable oil	60	mL
¹/₄	cup	red wine vinegar	60	mL
¹/₄	cup	granulated sugar	60	mL
1	tbsp.	toasted sesame seeds OR sunflower seeds	15	mL
1	tbsp.	minced onion	15	mL
1	tsp.	minced fresh dillweed	5	mL
1	tsp.	salt	5	mL
¹/₄	tsp.	garlic powder	1	mL
¹/₄	tsp.	pepper	1	mL
¹/₄	tsp.	dry hot mustard	1	mL
¹/₈	tsp.	cayenne pepper	0.5	mL

- Toss the sliced strawberries and spinach in a large salad bowl.
- **Dressing**: Combine the dressing ingredients in a small jar. Cover and shake until the ingredients are thoroughly combined.
- Just before serving, pour the dressing over the salad; toss well and serve immediately.

Variation:

- Use a 10 oz. (283 g) package of ready-to-use spinach.

Pictured on page 18.

STRAWBERRY SPINACH SALAD

A classic salad with a tangy/sweet dressing and many variation options.

Prep: 20 minutes   **Makes**: 4-6 servings
Required: large serving bowl

1¹/₂	cups	sliced fresh strawberries	375	mL
1		bunch fresh spinach, washed and dried	1	

ZESTY CIDER VINEGAR DRESSING:

¹/₄	cup	vegetable oil	60	mL
¹/₄	cup	granulated sugar	60	mL
2	tbsp.	cider vinegar	30	mL
2	tbsp.	Worcestershire sauce	30	mL
1	tbsp.	minced onion	15	mL
2	tsp.	poppy seeds	10	mL
¹/₄	tsp.	pepper	1	mL
¹/₄	tsp.	salt	1	mL

- Toss the sliced strawberries and spinach in a large salad bowl.
- **Dressing:** Combine the dressing ingredients in a small jar. Cover and shake until the ingredients are thoroughly combined.
- Just before serving, pour the dressing over the salad; toss well and serve immediately.
- Or, you can prepare individual salad plates and drizzle the dressing over each serving.

Variations:

- Use a 10 oz. (283 g) package of ready-to-use spinach.
- Cut some fresh asparagus into 2" (5 cm) lengths and cook until crisp-tender; drain and cool; add to the salad ingredients.
- Add 1 cup (250 mL) fresh blueberries to the salad.
- Add ¹/₂ cup (125 mL) toasted chopped pecans to the salad.
- Add ¹/₃ cup (75 mL), or more, crumbled blue or feta cheese to the salad.

STRAWBERRY POACHED SALMON

A quick and special meal – a light sauce with a sweet/tart flavor – perfect!

Prep: 40 minutes   **Cook**: 15 minutes   **Makes**: 4 servings
Required: large saucepan, medium skillet

4	cups	water	1	L
1		lemon, sliced	1	
1	tsp.	salt	5	mL
12		whole black peppercorns	12	
4		boneless salmon fillets, 6 oz. (180 g) each	4	

STRAWBERRY SAUCE:

1/2	cup	very thinly sliced onion	125	mL
1	tbsp.	butter	15	mL
1 1/4	cups	white wine	300	mL
2	tsp.	balsamic vinegar	10	mL
1/2	tsp.	salt	2	mL
1/4	tsp.	pepper	1	mL
1	tbsp.	granulated sugar	15	mL
2	tsp.	cornstarch	10	mL
1 1/2	cups	sliced fresh strawberries	375	mL
3	tbsp.	cold butter	45	mL

- Prepare the poaching liquid by bringing the water, lemon, salt and peppercorns to a boil in a large saucepan. Reduce the heat to a simmer and gently place 2 salmon fillets into the poaching liquid. **Simmer for 10-12 minutes for every 1" (2.5 cm) of salmon thickness**. Remove from the heat and keep warm. Repeat with the other 2 fillets.

- **Sauce:** Sauté the onion in the butter in a medium-sized skillet over medium heat just until soft – do not brown. Stir in the wine, balsamic vinegar, salt and pepper.

- Mix the sugar and cornstarch together in a small bowl; stir into the wine mixture. Gently bring to a boil, stirring constantly. Reduce the heat and gently simmer for another 1-2 minutes – the sauce will thicken a bit.

- Stir in the sliced strawberries and cook for 1-2 minutes, until just heated through. You do not want the strawberries to soften and loose their color.

- Stir in the additional cold butter until melted; remove from the heat.

- To serve, place the poached salmon on plates and spoon Strawberry Sauce over each serving.

SAUCY STRAWBERRY CHICKEN

A slightly spicy, tangy sauce with a delicate strawberry flavor. Delicious!

Preheat oven to 350°F (180°C).
Prep: 40 minutes   **Bake**: 1 hour   **Makes**: 4 servings
Required: large roasting pan   **Freeze**: suitable

ZESTY TOMATO SAUCE:

7¹/₂	oz.	can tomato sauce	213	mL
¹/₄	cup	honey	60	mL
¹/₄	cup	freshly squeezed orange juice	60	mL
1	tsp.	grated orange zest	5	mL
2	tsp.	Worcestershire sauce	10	mL
¹/₂	tsp.	dried red chili flakes, or more to taste	2	mL
¹/₄	tsp.	ground ginger	1	mL
¹/₂	tsp.	salt	2	mL
3-4	lb.	whole frying chicken, cut up	1.5-2	kg
²/₃	cup	diced onion	150	mL
2	tbsp.	butter	30	mL
4	cups	chopped, fresh strawberries	1	L

- **Sauce**: Combine the tomato sauce, honey, orange juice, orange zest, Worcestershire sauce, chili flakes, ginger and salt in a medium bowl. Set aside.
- Place the chicken pieces in a large roasting pan and set aside.
- Sauté the onion in butter in a medium saucepan until soft and translucent. Stir in the chopped strawberries and continue to cook for about 2 minutes, stirring frequently.
- Add the tomato sauce mixture to the saucepan; reduce the heat and simmer for about 5 minutes, stirring occasionally. Remove from the heat and pour over the chicken, stirring to distribute evenly.
- **Bake, uncovered, for 50-60 minutes**, or until the chicken is cooked through and the juices run clear. Stir occasionally.
- Serve with rice to absorb the delicious sauce.

STRAWBERRY CHICKEN STIR-FRY

Fast, easy and absolutely delicious – great for casual or company.

Prep: 30 minutes   **Cook**: 15 minutes   **Makes**: 4 servings
Required: large non-stick skillet

BALSAMIC HONEY SAUCE:

2	tbsp.	balsamic vinegar	30	mL
2	tbsp.	liquid honey	30	mL
2	tsp.	minced garlic	10	mL
2	tsp.	grated fresh ginger	10	mL
4	tsp.	soy sauce	20	mL
2	tbsp.	butter	30	mL
1	lb.	chicken breasts, cut into stir-fry strips salt and pepper	500	g
2	cups	sliced strawberries	500	mL

- **Sauce:** Combine the vinegar, honey, garlic, ginger and soy sauce in a small bowl. Set aside
- Melt the butter in a large skillet over medium heat. Quickly sauté the chicken strips until cooked through. Sprinkle with salt and pepper.
- Add the sauce and stir until the chicken is coated.
- Stir in the sliced strawberries. Continue to cook and stir for about 1-2 minutes, or until the strawberries are just heated through. Remove from the heat.
- Serve the chicken over rice with a green vegetable or spinach salad.

Variation:

- For a company presentation, use 4 skinless chicken breasts, pounded between sheets of waxed paper to flatten. Sauté until lightly browned and cooked through. Add the sauce. Stir to heat and then add the strawberries. Cook for about 1 minute more, or until just heated through. Serve with parslied rice.

Pictured on page 18.

STRAWBERRY-GLAZED CHOPS

Don't be put off by the ingredients or the quantities – this is delicious and fast!

Prep: 20 minutes   **Cook**: 15 minutes   **Makes**: 4 servings
Required: large non-stick skillet

GARLICKY STRAWBERRY SAUCE:

3/4	cup	strawberry jam (light spread-type)	175	mL
3	tbsp.	minced garlic	45	mL
3	tbsp.	soy sauce	45	mL
3	tbsp.	prepared horseradish	45	mL
1/3	cup	water	75	mL
2	tbsp.	butter	30	mL
8		pork loin chops, boneless (fast-fry)	8	
		salt and pepper to taste		
4		strawberries for garnish (optional)	4	

- **Sauce:** Combine the strawberry jam, garlic, soy sauce, horseradish and water. Cook over low heat, stirring frequently, until just heated through. Remove from the heat.
- Melt the butter in a large skillet. Sprinkle both sides of the chops lightly with salt and pepper and fry the chops quickly over medium heat until browned on both sides. Continue to cook until the juices run clear. Drain off all but 1 tbsp. (15 mL) butter and reduce the heat.
- Pour the sauce over the chops, stirring to scrape up the brown bits from the pan. Simmer for a just a few minutes, until the sauce thickens a bit.
- Serve the chops with rice (there is lots of sauce), and a green vegetable or salad. Garnish each plate with a fresh strawberry, if desired.

STRAWBERRY COBBLER

Simple comfort food – a tender flaky biscuit with a delicious sauce.

Preheat oven to 375°F (190°C).
Prep: 30 minutes   **Bake**: 25-30 minutes   **Makes**: 4-6 servings
Required: 2-3 quart (2-3 L) baking dish, greased

STRAWBERRY SAUCE:

1/2	cup	granulated sugar	125	mL
3	tbsp.	cornstarch	45	mL
1 1/3	cups	water	325	mL
1	tsp.	grated lemon zest	5	mL
4	cups	halved, fresh strawberries OR frozen berries	1	L
2	tbsp.	butter	30	mL

DROP BISCUIT DOUGH:

1 1/4	cups	all-purpose flour	300	mL
3	tbsp.	granulated sugar	45	mL
1	tbsp.	baking powder	15	mL
1	tsp.	grated lemon zest (optional)	5	mL
1/4	tsp.	salt	1	mL
1/3	cup	butter	75	mL
1/2	cup	milk	125	mL
1		egg, slightly beaten	1	
2	tsp.	granulated sugar (optional)	10	mL

- **Sauce:** Combine the sugar and cornstarch in a medium saucepan. Stir in the water and lemon zest; cook over medium heat, stirring constantly, until thickened and clear. Remove from the heat.
- Add the strawberries and butter; stir until the butter is melted. Pour into the prepared baking dish.
- **Biscuit Dough:** Combine the flour, sugar, baking **powder**, lemon zest and salt. Cut in the butter until the mixture resembles coarse crumbs. Add the milk and egg and mix quickly, until no trace of flour remains.
- Drop the batter by large spoonfuls onto the Strawberry Sauce (about 6 large dollops). Sprinkle with sugar if you wish.
- **Bake for 25-30 minutes,** or until the biscuits are lightly browned. Remove and cool slightly. Serve warm or cool.

Variations:
- Use a mixture of half strawberries and half sliced peaches or nectarines.
- Use half strawberries and half sliced rhubarb; use 3/4 cup (175 mL) sugar.

STRAWBERRY SOUR CREAM CAKE

Simple and not too sweet, with a lemony sour cream topping.

Preheat oven to 350°F (180°C).
Prep: 30 minutes   **Bake**: 70-75 minutes   **Makes**: 8-10 servings
Required: 10" (25 cm) springform pan, greased

1¹/₂	cups	all-purpose flour	375	mL
¹/₄	cup	granulated sugar	60	mL
1¹/₂	tsp.	baking powder	7	mL
¹/₄	tsp.	salt	1	mL
¹/₂	cup	softened butter	125	mL
1	tsp.	vanilla extract	5	mL
1		egg, beaten	1	
4	cups	sliced fresh strawberries	1	L
3	tbsp.	granulated sugar	45	mL
2	tsp.	grated lemon zest	10	mL
2	cups	sour cream	500	mL
¹/₃	cup	granulated sugar	75	mL
2	tbsp.	freshly squeezed lemon juice	30	mL
2		egg yolks	2	

- Combine the flour, sugar, baking **powder** and salt in a medium bowl.
- Stir the butter, vanilla and beaten egg into the flour mixture; work with your hands until all of the ingredients are evenly combined. Pat into the bottom of the springform pan.
- Combine the sliced strawberries, sugar and lemon zest in a separate bowl. Sprinkle evenly over the crust in the pan.
- Beat the sour cream, sugar, lemon juice and egg yolks in a medium bowl, with an electric mixer, until thoroughly combined. Pour evenly over the berries.
- **Bake for 70-75 minutes**, or until firm and golden brown on top. Remove from the oven and cool on a wire rack before serving.
- Store in the refrigerator if not serving immediately.

STRAWBERRY SHORTCAKES

Simple is sometimes best! Use the best ripe flavorful berries for this recipe.

Preheat oven to 425°F (220°C).
Prep: 40 minutes   **Bake**: 11-12 minutes   **Makes**: 8-10 servings
Required: baking sheets, ungreased

STRAWBERRY TOPPING:

1/3	cup	granulated sugar	75	mL
1/4	cup	boiling water	60	mL
2	tbsp.	Grand Marnier (optional)	30	mL
4	cups	sliced fresh strawberries	1	L

SHORTCAKES:

2 1/4	cups	all-purpose flour	560	mL
2	tbsp.	granulated sugar	30	mL
1	tbsp.	baking powder	15	mL
1/2	tsp.	salt	2	mL
1/2	cup	cold shortening (Crisco)	125	mL
3/4	cup	buttermilk	175	mL
1		egg	1	
1	tsp.	finely grated lemon zest	5	mL
2	tbsp.	granulated sugar (for sprinkling)	30	mL

WHIPPED CREAM TOPPING:

1 1/2	cups	whipping cream	375	mL
1/3	cup	sour cream	75	mL
2-3	tbsp.	granulated sugar	30-45	mL
1	tsp.	vanilla extract	5	mL

- **Topping**: Dissolve the sugar in the boiling water in a measuring cup and then stir in the Grand Marnier. Set aside for a few minutes to cool.

- Place the sliced strawberries in a medium bowl and add the cooled sugar mixture; let sit at room temperature for 30 minutes, stirring occasionally.

- **Shortcakes**: Combine the flour, sugar, baking **powder** and salt in a medium bowl. Cut in the shortening with a pastry blender until the mixture resembles coarse crumbs.

STRAWBERRY SHORTCAKES
continued

- Whisk the buttermilk, egg and lemon zest together until well blended; pour into the flour mixture. Stir until combined and turn the dough onto a floured surface. Knead 3-4 times and pat into a circle. Roll the dough to a ³/₄" (2.0 cm) thickness.

- Cut the dough into circles with a 3" (8 cm) round cutter. Gather leftover dough, re-roll and continue making more circles until all the dough is used.

- Place the dough circles on an ungreased baking sheet; brush with a little water and sprinkle the additional granulated sugar on top.

- **Bake for 11-12 minutes,** or until lightly browned. Remove and cool slightly on a wire rack.

- **Topping:** Whip the cream until very stiff peaks form. Add the sour cream, sugar and vanilla and continue to beat gently at low speed until just combined.

- **To Serve:** Split the shortcakes in half horizontally while still warm. Spoon the strawberry topping and juices on the bottom halves and then cover with some whipped cream. Place the shortcake tops on the cream and spoon on more berries, finishing with a large dollop of cream.

Variations:

- If you like larger biscuits, use a 4" (10 cm.) cookie cutter. You will have fewer biscuits (about 6). Or you can roll out the dough and cut into squares.

- Use 2 x 15 oz. (425 g) pkgs. frozen, sliced strawberries in light syrup instead of fresh strawberries. Add 1-2 tbsp. (15-30 mL) Grand Marnier to the thawed strawberries and juice or stir in 1-2 tsp. (5-10 mL) finely grated orange zest.

- Substitute some chopped peaches or nectarines for a portion of the strawberries.

- **Easy Version:** Instead of rolling and cutting the dough, drop mounds of dough directly from a large spoon onto the cookie sheet.

BERRY-LICIOUS CHEESECAKE

Fresh great strawberry flavor – light tasting, this can be enjoyed year round.

Prep: 40 minutes   **Chill**: 4-6 hours   **Makes**: 8-10 servings
Required: 9" (23 cm) springform pan

1 1/2	cups	graham cracker crumbs	375	mL
1/4	cup	granulated sugar	60	mL
1/3	cup	melted butter	75	mL
1/4	oz.	pkg. gelatin powder (1 envelope)	7.5	g
1/4	cup	cold water	60	mL
8	oz.	pkg. cream cheese, softened	250	g
1/2	cup	granulated sugar	125	mL
15	oz.	pkg. frozen strawberries in syrup, thawed	425	g
1	cup	whipping cream	250	mL

- Combine the crumbs, sugar and melted butter in a small bowl; press into the bottom of a springform pan. Set aside.
- Sprinkle the gelatin over the cold water in a very small saucepan; set over low heat until dissolved. Cool to room temperature.
- Beat the cream cheese and sugar in a separate bowl, with an electric mixer, until smooth.
- Drain the thawed strawberries well, save the juice and reserve the strawberries for later. Measure the strawberry juice and **add enough water to make 1 cup (250 mL)**.
- Slowly beat the strawberry juice and the softened gelatin into the cream cheese mixture.
- Place in the refrigerator and cool until slightly thickened (like unbeaten egg whites).
- Whip the cream until stiff peaks form. Gently fold the whipped cream and the reserved sliced strawberries into the slightly thickened cream cheese mixture.
- Pour the strawberry filling over the crust and **chill until firm, about 4-6 hours**.
- Garnish individual servings with additional whipped cream and fresh strawberries, if desired.

STRAWBERRY TIRAMISU

Rich – traditional, with a twist – a perfect grand finale.

Prep: 40 minutes   **Cool:** 6-8 hours   **Makes:** 4-6 servings
Required: 8" (20 cm) glass baking pan

STRAWBERRY COULIS:

15	oz.	pkg. frozen sliced strawberries in syrup	425	g

TIRAMISU:

18		ladyfingers, 1 x 4" (2.5 x 10 cm) size	18	
1/3	cup	espresso OR strong coffee, chilled	75	mL
2	tbsp.	brandy	30	mL
1	cup	mascarpone cheese	250	mL
1/2	cup	whipping cream	125	mL
1/4	cup	berry sugar	60	mL
2	tbsp.	brandy	30	mL
1	cup	diced, fresh strawberries	250	mL
1	cup	whipping cream	250	mL
2	tbsp.	berry sugar	30	mL
		unsweetened cocoa powder for sprinkling (optional)		

- **Coulis:** Purée the thawed strawberries in syrup until very smooth; set aside.
- **Tiramisu:** Arrange half the ladyfingers in 1 layer in the baking dish, breaking to fit if necessary. Stir the espresso and brandy together and brush half of the liquid over the ladyfingers.
- Combine the mascarpone cheese, cream, sugar and brandy and beat, with an electric mixer, until completely smooth and creamy. Stir in the diced fresh strawberries.
- Spread half of the strawberry mixture over the ladyfingers and smooth. Top with the remaining ladyfingers; brush with the remaining coffee mixture; cover with the remaining strawberry mixture.
- Whip the cream until stiff; add sugar and beat a few minutes more. Spread over the cheese mixture. Chill for at least 6 hours.
- Just before serving, dust lightly with a bit of unsweetened cocoa powder.
- **To serve:** Pour some strawberry coulis onto each serving plate and place a piece of tiramisu on the coulis. Garnish with a fresh strawberry.

Note:

- If you can't find mascarpone cheese, beat 8 oz. (250 g) cream cheese, room temperature, with 1/4 cup (60 mL) sour cream and 2 tbsp. (30 mL) whipping cream or butter.

■

STRAWBERRY PINEAPPLE SAUCE

Wonderful served over ice cream or over plain yogurt.

Prep: 20 minutes   **Cook**: 15 minutes   **Makes**: 3¹/₂ cups (875 mL)
Required: medium saucepan

10¹/₂ oz.		pkg. frozen whole strawberries, thawed with juices	300	g
14	oz.	can crushed pineapple, undrained	398	mL
1	tbsp.	freshly squeezed lemon juice	15	mL
2	tsp.	grated lemon zest	10	mL
¹/₃	cup	granulated sugar	75	mL
4	tsp.	cornstarch	20	mL

- Purée the thawed strawberries and any juices (you should have 1¹/₂ cups/375 mL of purée). Place in the saucepan and mix in the undrained crushed pineapple, lemon juice and lemon zest.
- Combine the sugar and cornstarch in a small bowl and stir into the strawberry mixture.
- Cook over medium heat, stirring until thickened. Remove from the heat and cool.

STRAWBERRY SAUCE

This easy sauce is wonderful over ice cream, pound cake
or as a coulis for other desserts.

Prep: 10 minutes   **Required**: blender   **Makes**: 1³/₄ cups (425 mL)

15	oz.	pkg. frozen, sliced strawberries in light syrup	425	g
1	tbsp.	freshly squeezed lemon juice	15	mL
2	tbsp.	cherry brandy, Kirsch OR Grand Marnier	30	mL
1-2	tbsp.	granulated sugar, to taste (optional)	15-30	mL
2	tsp.	finely grated lemon OR orange zest (optional)	10	mL

- Place thawed strawberries, lemon juice and liqueur in a blender and purée until smooth. Taste and add additional sugar, if required, and lemon zest.

CHOCOLATE STRAWBERRY SAUCE

Strawberries and chocolate are perfect together!

Prep: 30 minutes   **Cook**: 10 minutes   **Makes**: 4 servings
Required: medium skillet

2	cups	sliced, fresh strawberries	500	mL
3	tbsp.	butter	45	mL
1/3	cup	coarsely chopped walnuts	75	mL
3	tbsp.	brown sugar	45	mL
1	oz.	semisweet chocolate, grated (1 square)	30	g
2	tbsp.	freshly squeezed orange juice	30	mL

- Prepare the strawberries and set aside.
- Melt the butter in the skillet over medium heat; add the walnuts. Cook and stir for 1-2 minutes, until frothy.
- Stir in the brown sugar, cooking and stirring for just a few seconds. Remove the pan from the heat.
- Immediately add the grated chocolate, orange juice and sliced strawberries. Stir to melt the chocolate and coat the strawberries.
- Serve the sauce warm, spooned over vanilla ice cream, crêpes or waffles.

Variations:

- Instead of orange juice, use Grand Marnier, Cointreau or Triple Sec.
- Use chopped pecans instead of walnuts.

STRAWBERRY-ORANGE COMPÔTE

The cardamom is a must, it adds a wonderful flavor – a favorite!

Prep: 30 minutes   **Chill**: 1-2 hours   **Makes**: 4-6 servings
Required: medium bowl

3	cups	sliced, fresh strawberries	750	mL
3		navel oranges	3	
1/4	cup	freshly squeezed orange juice	60	mL
1	tsp.	finely grated orange zest	5	mL
2	tbsp.	liquid honey	30	mL
1/2	tsp.	ground cardamom	2	mL

- Prepare the strawberries and place in the bowl.
- Grate the orange zest, then slice off the top and bottom of each orange. Cut off the peel in vertical strips, making sure that no white pith or membrane remains.
- Then, cut between each membrane to obtain the orange segments. Cut the segments into smaller pieces. Place the orange segments, along with any of the juices, in the bowl with the strawberries.
- Combine the additional orange juice, orange zest, honey and cardamom. Pour over the strawberries and oranges and stir well.
- Place the compote in the refrigerator for 1-2 hours to blend the flavors and let the juices form. Stir occasionally.
- Serve as a sauce over vanilla ice cream, serve "as-is" for breakfast or brunch, or warm slightly and serve as a sauce over waffles or French Toast.

Strawberries & Wine, page 41
Chocolate Dipped Strawberries, page 40
Russian Cream & Romanoff Strawberries, page 44

FRESH STRAWBERRY PIE

This captures the best – a delightfully fresh-tasting pie with a beautiful red color.

Preheat oven to 350°F (180°C).
Prep: 40 minutes   **Bake:** 6-7 minutes   **Makes:** 8 servings
Required: 9" (23 cm) pie plate   **Chill:** 2-3 hours

SHORTBREAD CRUST

2	cups	crushed shortbread cookies	500	mL
1/4	cup	finely chopped almonds	60	mL
1/3	cup	melted butter	75	mL

STRAWBERRY FILLING:

15	oz.	pkg. frozen sliced strawberries in light syrup	425	g
1 1/4	cups	cranberry juice OR water	300	mL
1/3	cup	cornstarch, plus 1 tbsp.	90	mL
1/4	cup	granulated sugar	60	mL
1 1/2	tsp.	finely grated orange OR lemon zest	7	mL
5	cups	halved, quartered, or thickly sliced fresh, ripe strawberries	1.25	L
2	cups	whipping cream, whipped	250	mL

- **Crust:** Combine the cookie crumbs, almonds and butter in a bowl. Press on the bottom and sides of the pie plate. **Bake for 6-7 minutes.** Remove and cool. (Or use a graham cracker or prebaked pastry crust.)
- **Filling:** Place the thawed berries in syrup in a blender. Cover and purée. Add juice to equal 3 cups (750 mL) of liquid. Place in a saucepan.
- Combine the cornstarch and sugar; whisk into the berries. Cook over medium heat, stirring constantly, until thickened and clear. Remove from the heat and stir in the orange zest. Cool slightly.
- Stir the fresh strawberries into the strawberry sauce until well coated.
- Pour the strawberries into the pie crust; chill for 2-3 hours, or until set.
- To serve, top each slice of pie with whipped cream.

Variation:

- Add 2 tbsp. (30 mL) of brandy instead of the grated zest.
- Divide the sauce and berries in half. Combine one half of each and pour into the crust. Arrange the remaining berries on top in a decorative pattern and brush with the remaining sauce.

Fresh Strawberry Pie, pictured opposite
Strawberry Cream Amaretto, page 9

OLD-FASHIONED STRAWBERRY PIE

The ultimate strawberry pie – unlike any other. This will be your favorite!

Preheat oven to 400°F (200°C).
Prep: 35 minutes   **Bake**: 1 hour   **Makes**: 8 servings
Required: 9" (23 cm) pie plate

pastry for a 9" (23 cm) single-crust pie

CRUMB TOPPING:

3/4	cup	granulated sugar	175	mL
3/4	cup	all-purpose flour	175	mL
1/8	tsp.	ground nutmeg	0.5	mL
1/4	tsp.	salt	1	mL
1/3	cup	butter, plus 1 tbsp.	90	mL

STRAWBERRY FILLING:

5	cups	halved fresh strawberries	1.25	L
1/2	cup	granulated sugar	125	mL
1/2	cup	all-purpose flour	125	mL
1	tbsp.	cornstarch	15	mL

TOPPING:

3-4	tbsp.	butter	45-60	mL
3	tbsp.	granulated sugar	45	mL

- **Crumb Topping:** Combine the sugar, flour, nutmeg and salt in a medium bowl. Cut in the butter with a pastry blender until the mixture resembles coarse crumbs. Set aside.
- **Filling:** Prepare the strawberries and place in a large bowl. Set aside.
- Combine the sugar, flour and cornstarch in a small bowl. Gently stir into the berries, coating them well – be careful not to crush them.
- Pour the berries and coating mixture into the pie crust, distributing evenly, mounding a bit in the center. If the pie seems full, they will compress as they bake.
- Spread the crumb topping over the berries, covering the filling out to the edges. Dot the crumb mixture with small pieces of the additional butter and wrap the edges of the pie crust with strips of foil to prevent burning.
- **Bake for 20 minutes. Reduce heat to 375°F (190°C) and bake for another 40 minutes** (1 hour in all).
- During the last 10 minutes, sprinkle 3 tbsp. (45 mL) of sugar over the pie and finish baking. Remove from the oven and cool on a wire rack.
- Serve plain, with vanilla ice cream or with a dollop of whipped cream.

DIPPED STRAWBERRIES

Simple and delicious – quite possibly one of the best ways to enjoy strawberries!

Prep: 20 minutes   **Makes**: 4-6 servings
Required: *large dessert bowl, small bowls for dipping*

| 2 | lbs. | fresh, ripe strawberries | 1 | kg |
| 2/3 | cup | sour cream | 150 | mL |

DIPPING SUGGESTIONS:

> golden or Demerara sugar
> crushed cookie crumbs (e.g., ginger, vanilla wafers, etc.)
> walnuts, pecans, almonds, etc., finely chopped
> grated semisweet chocolate
> toasted shredded coconut
> plain shredded coconut
> toffee bits

- Select the freshest rich red strawberries you can find for this easy dessert.
- Gently rinse the strawberries and pat dry, leaving on the hulls and/or stems. Place the berries in a large dessert bowl.
- Place the sour cream in a small bowl.
- Select any of the additional dipping ingredients and place each of them in separate small bowls.
- Grasp the strawberries by the hull or stem; dip into the sour cream and then into any of the dipping suggestions above and enjoy! Let your guests have fun creating their favorite combinations.

CHOCOLATE-DIPPED STRAWBERRIES

Simple and delicious – quite possibly one of the best ways to enjoy strawberries!

Prep: 20 minutes   **Chill**: 15-20 minutes   **Makes**: 4-6 serving
Required: large baking sheet lined with waxed paper

18-24	fresh, ripe strawberries	18-24	
8 ozs.	semisweet, milk or bittersweet chocolate (8 squares) OR 1¹/₂ cups (325 mL) chocolate chips	250	g

DIPPING SUGGESTIONS (optional):

crushed cookie crumbs (e.g., ginger, vanilla wafers, etc.)
walnuts, pecans, almonds, etc., finely chopped
toasted or plain shredded coconut
toffee bits

- Select the freshest rich red strawberries – medium to large are best.
- Gently rinse the strawberries and pat dry, leaving on the hulls or stems. It is ESSENTIAL that berries have NO water on them.
- Melt the chocolate in a microwave for 30 second intervals, until almost melted, stir to melt completely, OR melt over very low heat or in a double boiler. Watch carefully and stir thoroughly. Remove from the heat. Set the melted chocolate in a larger shallow pan of hot water to maintain the dipping consistency. No water must touch the chocolate.
- Grasp each strawberry by the hull or spear with a toothpick and dip into the chocolate until ²/₃ of the berry is coated. Allow excess chocolate to drip off; place coated strawberries on waxed paper (remove the toothpick if used).
- **Optional**: After excess chocolate has dripped off, roll berries in toppings – leave some of the chocolate area plain. Place on waxed paper.
- Refrigerate for 15-20 minutes to firm the chocolate. Let the berries stand at room temperature for about 10 minutes before serving.

Variation:
- Melt 6 squares of white chocolate in a microwave, over very low heat or in a double boiler. Watch carefully and stir – remove from the heat and keep warm. Dip strawberries as above or you can "double dip" – once in white chocolate (chill to firm) and then dip just 1 side of the berry in semisweet chocolate. Or dip in 1 type, chill to set and drizzle another chocolate over the top – have fun!

Note:
- Use the best-quality chocolate to get the best flavor.

Pictured on page 35.

STRAWBERRIES & WINE

Elegant and fabulous – your guests will be fighting for the wine in their glasses!

Prep: 20 minutes   **Chill**: 2-3 hours   **Makes**: 4 servings
Required: medium glass bowl, 4 beautiful dessert dishes or stemmed glasses

4	cups	sliced, fresh ripe strawberries	1	L
1	cup	granulated sugar	250	mL
2	cups	dry white wine	500	mL

- Place the sliced strawberries into the glass bowl.
- Stir the sugar and the wine into the strawberries; continue stirring for a few minutes.
- Cover with plastic wrap and place in the refrigerator for about 3 hours to marinate, stirring occasionally to mix the berries and wine. The sugar will be completed dissolved at the end of this time.
- To serve, spoon the berries into individual dessert dishes and then divide the remaining "strawberry-wine" among the dishes.

Variation:

- **Ginger Wine Berries**: Reduce the sugar to $1/4$ cup (60 mL) and add $1 1/2$ tsp. (7 mL) finely grated fresh ginger root. Stir to combine; cover and refrigerate for 2-3 hours to blend the flavors, stirring occasionally.

Pictured on page 35.

BALSAMIC STRAWBERRIES

Sophisticated and tasty. Italians often enjoy berries with balsamic vinegar.

Prep: 20 minutes   **Makes**: 4 servings
Required: medium-sized bowl

4	cups	sliced fresh ripe strawberries	1	L
3	tbsp.	packed brown sugar	45	mL
1	tbsp.	balsamic vinegar	15	mL
1/4	tsp.	black pepper	1	mL

- Place the sliced strawberries in a bowl and stir in the brown sugar. Let stand for 10-15 minutes to let the juices form; stir occasionally.
- Stir the balsamic vinegar and pepper into the strawberries until combined.
- **For a Dessert**: Spoon these wonderful strawberries and juices over ice cream or a slice of plain poundcake, with a small dollop of whipped cream, and enjoy a different and tasty dessert. Or spoon the berries and juices into individual bowls and enjoy "as-is."
- **For a Salad**: Arrange red leaf lettuce or a combination of lettuce and spinach leaves on each of 4 plates. Divide the strawberries and juices among the plates and enjoy a wonderful salad.

STRAWBERRIES & AMARETTO CREAM

Incredibly simple and wonderful. Use the best ripe, fresh strawberries!

Prep: 15 minutes   **Makes**: 4 servings
Required: 4 dessert dishes

3/4	cup	sour cream	175	mL
3	tbsp.	icing (confectioner's) sugar	45	mL
2-3	tbsp.	amaretto liqueur	30-45	mL
3	cups	sliced, fresh strawberries	750	mL
2	tbsp.	sliced toasted almonds for garnish (optional)	30	mL

- Combine the sour cream, icing sugar and amaretto in a small bowl.
- **To serve**, spoon sliced strawberries into 4 dessert dishes; top generously with the sour cream mixture. Sprinkle each serving with sliced almonds.

STRAWBERRIES & GRAND MARNIER

A little expensive but elegant. If you get into it first, your guests will never see it.

Prep: 30 minutes   **Chill**: 1-2 hours.   **Makes**: 4-6 servings
Required: double boiler, large dessert bowl or 4-6 dessert dishes

5		egg yolks	5	
1	cup	berry sugar	250	mL
1	cup	Grand Marnier liqueur	250	mL
1	cup	whipping cream	250	mL
4	cups	quartered, fresh ripe strawberries	1	L

- Beat the egg yolks in a medium bowl, with an electric mixer, until lemon colored. Add the berry sugar and continue beating until thick and a light creamy yellow color (about 2 minutes).
- Slowly beat in the liqueur (1 cup/250 mL is correct) at low speed. Transfer the mixture to the top pan of the double boiler.
- Cook over medium heat, stirring constantly (don't even think about not stirring this mixture), until the custard thickens and coats a spoon. This takes about 4 minutes – do not let the custard come to a boil. Remove from the heat immediately and cool.
- Whip the cream until stiff peaks form. Fold the cream into the cooled custard until smooth, with no streaks remaining.
- Refrigerate until ready to use.
- Spoon the strawberries into individual dessert dishes and pour the sauce over each serving.

Variation:

- Use any other orange-flavored liqueur or brandy, e.g., Triple Sec, Cointreau, etc.

RUSSIAN CREAM & ROMANOFF STRAWBERRIES

Creamy, sophisticated, simple. This tastes absolutely heavenly!

Prep: 35 minutes   **Chill**: 4-6 hours or overnight   **Makes**: 4-6 servings
Required: 1-quart (1 L) dessert bowl or 4-6 stemmed glasses

RUSSIAN CREAM:

$^2/_3$	cup	granulated sugar	150	mL
$^1/_4$	oz.	pkg. gelatin powder (1 envelope)	7.5	g
$^1/_2$	cup	cold water	125	mL
1	cup	whipping cream	250	mL
$1^1/_2$	cups	sour cream	375	mL
1	tsp.	vanilla extract	5	mL

ROMANOFF STRAWBERRIES:

4	cups	sliced, fresh strawberries	1	L
$^1/_2$	cup	granulated sugar	125	mL
2	tbsp.	vodka	30	mL
2	tbsp.	Grand Marnier	30	mL
2	tbsp.	rum	30	mL

- Combine the sugar and gelatin powder in a medium saucepan. Stir in the cold water; let stand for 5 minutes to soften.
- Cook over medium heat, stirring constantly, until it just begins to boil. Remove from the heat.
- Slowly stir the whipping cream into the hot mixture. Whisk in the sour cream and vanilla and stir until smooth and creamy.
- Pour into a dessert bowl. If using stemmed glasses or individual dessert dishes, leave about 1" (2.5 cm) or more headspace for the sauce. Cover and chill for 4-6 hours or overnight.
- **Romanoff Strawberries:** Combine the sliced strawberries, sugar, vodka, Grand Marnier and rum in a bowl and stir well. Chill, stirring occasionally.
- **To Serve:** Spoon the Russian Cream into dessert dishes and top with Romanoff Strawberries and some juices. Or, if already in individual glasses or dessert dishes, just top with berries and juices.

Variation:

- If you don't have all of the liquors and liqueurs, purchase the tiny bottles or use a combination of what you have hand.

Pictured on page 35.

RUM-BERRY MOUSSE

A perfect ending – light and refreshing!

Prep: 30 minutes   **Cool**: 2-4 hours   **Makes**: 6–8 servings
Required: 2-quart (2 L) serving bowl or 6-8 individual stemmed glasses

2x^1/$_4$ oz.	pkgs. gelatin powder (2 envelopes)	2x7.5	g
^{1}/$_3$ cup	cold water	75	mL
10^1/$_2$ oz.	pkg. frozen whole strawberries, thawed OR 1^1/$_3$ cups purée (325 mL)	300	g
^{3}/$_4$ cup	granulated sugar	175	mL
^{1}/$_2$ cup	rum	125	mL
1^1/$_2$ cups	whipping cream	375	mL
	sliced fresh strawberries for garnish		

- Sprinkle the gelatin over the cold water in a very small saucepan. Set over low heat until dissolved. Cool to room temperature.
- Purée the strawberries and juices (you should have 1^1/$_3$ cups/325 mL). If you don't, add a bit of water to make up the difference. Place in a medium-sized bowl and add the sugar, stirring until dissolved.
- Stir the cooled gelatin into the purée and combine thoroughly. Cool in the refrigerator until it starts to set (as thick as unbeaten egg whites).
- Remove the strawberry mixture from the refrigerator and stir in the rum.
- Whip the cream until stiff peaks form. Gently fold into the strawberry mixture until no streaks of white remain.
- Pour the mousse into a serving bowl or individual glasses and refrigerate until firm. Garnish each serving with a sliced fresh strawberry.

Variation:

- Use ripe fresh strawberries. Purée enough strawberries to measure 1^1/$_3$ cups (325 mL) and proceed as above.

Note:

- To make a strawberry fan garnish, slice strawberries vertically, from just below the hull or leaves through the tip, making sure the hull end is intact. Twist the strawberry slightly to "open" the fan.

STRAWBERRY ICE CREAM

Absolutely the most delicious, fresh strawberry flavor.

Prep: 40 minutes   **Cool**: 2 hours or overnight   **Makes**: 2 quarts (2 L)
Required: medium saucepan, 2-quart (2 L) ice-cream maker   **Freeze**: required

1¹/₃ cups	mashed fresh strawberries	325	mL
2¹/₄ cups	whipping cream	550	mL
³/₄ cup	berry sugar	175	mL
1¹/₂ tsp.	fresh lemon juice	7	mL
¹/₈ tsp.	salt	0.5	mL

- Combine the strawberries, cream, sugar, lemon juice and salt in a large bowl and stir thoroughly.
- At this point you can chill the mixture for a few hours or overnight or you can proceed.
- Pour the strawberry mixture into the ice cream maker and freeze according to the manufacturer's directions.
- Serve the ice cream plain or pour some strawberry liqueur over or serve with any of the sauces in this book, see pages 32, 33, 34.

Variations:

- Off-season, use frozen whole strawberries (not in syrup). Place partially thawed strawberries and their juice in a blender and "chop" or "mix" for only a few seconds – do not purée. Lumps of berries are nice in the ice cream. Proceed as above.
- Substitute half-and-half cream for the whipping cream, or use whole milk. The consistency/texture of the ice cream will be a little different.

STRAWBERRY-RASPBERRY FREEZER JAM

An incredible bright red color, fresh flavor and easy to make in- or off-season.

Prep: 30 minutes   **Cook**: 5 minutes   **Makes**: about 5 cups (1.25 L)
Required: 5, 1-cup (250 mL) freezer containers   **Freezing**: required

2	cups	crushed fresh strawberries	500	mL
1	cup	crushed fresh raspberries	250	mL
1-2	tsp.	finely grated orange OR lemon zest	5-10	mL
4	cups	granulated sugar	1	L
3/4	cup	water	175	mL
2	oz.	pkg. powdered fruit pectin (not light)	57	g

- Combine the strawberries, raspberries, orange zest and sugar in a large bowl; stir until all the sugar is absorbed. Let stand for 10-15 minutes.
- Mix the water and the fruit pectin in a small saucepan until combined. Bring to a boil over medium heat, stirring constantly. Stir and boil for 1 minute.
- Remove the pectin mixture from the heat and stir into the crushed fruit; stir for 3 minutes.
- Pour the jam into individual freezer containers; cover and let stand on the counter for 24 hours. Store in the freezer.

Variations:

- Instead of the lemon or orange zest, add 1 tsp. (5 mL) of ground cinnamon.
- This is a great use for your summer-frozen berries. Just partially thaw the berries and pour into a blender with all of the juices. Cover and chop or stir for just a few seconds, until the berries are crushed and some lumps remain. Do not purée.

Note:

- The texture of freezer jam is slightly less firm than that of traditional jams.

FREEZING STRAWBERRIES

Freezing is one of the simplest ways to preserve strawberries, capturing and preserving them at the height of summer sweetness and at the most economical time of year. Freezing preserves food by stopping the growth of bacteria, not by destroying it, so proper technique ensures flavor and nutrient value is retained. Although frozen strawberries keep their flavor and color, the texture changes and they become softer and a bit mushy. So, when choosing the freezing method, keep in mind their intended use. Although many recipes can easily incorporate frozen berries, some are best made using only fresh. If you plan on using frozen berries for specific recipes, pack the berries in premeasured amounts just right for the specific recipe.

Selecting and Washing Berries

Strawberries are best frozen soon after harvesting. Choose berries that are fully ripe, bright red in color, firm and aromatic. Underripe berries may be bitter and overripe berries are best frozen as purées. Because **freezing does not improve quality**, freeze berries at the stage they would taste best when eaten fresh, keeping in mind the following:

- Leave the hulls on until after the berries are washed and drained.
- Do not let the berries "soak" as they tend to absorb water quickly, making for a poor frozen product. Instead, gently and quickly rinse berries in cold water several times to remove dirt, bacteria and residues.
- Immediately drain berries in a colander or on towels; remove the hulls.
- Sort out and discard bruised, decayed or underripe berries.
- Work with smaller, more manageable, quantities of berries at a time – it is easier and helps prevent loss of quality during the freezing process.

Freezing/Packaging Containers

Proper containers will protect the berries from drying out (freezer burn), prevent flavors in the freezer from mixing, and ensure a high-quality frozen product. Containers should be moisture and vapor-proof and easy to seal. Choose containers or plastic bags specifically designed for frozen foods.

Ascorbic Acid

Not required for strawberries, but useful in preserving color and flavor, ascorbic acid is typically added to syrups and sugar-packed fruits prior to freezing. It is sold under a few names in the canning section of grocery stores. Follow the manufacturer's directions provided.

Thawing Berries

Frozen berries are better with slow defrosting in the refrigerator and used/eaten when there are just a very few ice crystals left.

Freezing Methods

There are several methods of "packing" strawberries for freezing: open freeze, dry pack (no sugar), dry sugar pack, or syrup pack. While berries have a better texture if they are packed in sugar or syrup, sugar is not required to preserve them. Berries packed in sugar or syrup are best for uncooked desserts, sauces, or eating as is; frozen whole berries are best for cooking because there is less liquid present on thawing.

Tray Pack (open freeze): Good for small, ripe whole berries – providing good-quality frozen berries without added sugar. Spread the washed and dried berries in a single layer on baking trays lined with waxed paper, allowing air space around each berry. Place in the freezer uncovered. When the fruit is hard (you can leave it overnight), package into freezer bags in the quantities you prefer. Remove as much air as possible, allowing no headspace, and return to the freezer.

Dry Pack (no sugar): Pack individual whole or sliced berries directly into containers; seal and freeze. Purée extra-ripe berries and freeze in premeasured amounts for sauces and beverages.

Dry Sugar Pack: Good for juicy, ripe berries – sugar draws the juices from the berries providing a sweetened liquid in which to freeze them. Slice or crush berries in a large bowl; sprinkle with sugar to taste. Stir occasionally until the sugar is dissolved and juices form. Pack into containers, leaving 1/2" (1.3 cm) headspace. Seal and freeze immediately.

Dry pack Formula: For each 4 cups (I L) of sliced berries add 3/4 cup (175 mL) of sugar. Sprinkle the sugar over the berries and stir.

Syrup Pack: Best if the fruit is to be used as an uncooked dessert (eaten "as-is"). The proportion of sugar used depends on how sweet you prefer the berries and can range from a light syrup for mild-flavored fruits to a very heavy syrup for sour fruits. Generally, a light syrup is adequate for strawberries. It is not necessary to boil the syrup mixture, just stir until all the sugar is dissolved (if using hot water, cool before using).

Light Syrup: 1 3/4 cups (425 mL) granulated sugar to 4 cups (1 L) water
Medium Syrup: 2 3/4 cups (675 mL) granulated sugar to 4 cups (1 L) water
Heavy Syrup: 4 cups (1 L) granulated sugar to 4 cups (1 L) water

Pour 1/2 cup (125 mL) of cold syrup into the container, add the sliced berries and cover with additional syrup, leaving at least 1/2" (1.3 cm) headspace. To keep the fruit from floating, place a small piece of crumpled waxed paper on top and press into the liquid. Seal and freeze.

COMMON SUBSTITUTIONS

While these are acceptable substitutions "in a pinch," note that when substituting ingredients some will work very well and some will have an impact on the final product. Never expect to get exactly the same results as you would if using the called-for ingredient. If a specific ingredient is key to a recipe, it's probably best to wait until you have it on hand.

ITEM	QUANTITY	SUBSTITUTION
Allspice	1 tsp./5 mL	$1/2$ tsp. (2 mL) cinnamon plus $1/8$ tsp. (0.5 mL) cloves
Buttermilk	1 cup/250 mL	1 cup (250 mL) plain yogurt OR sour milk
Capers		chopped green olives OR dill pickles
Chocolate (unsweetened)	1 oz./30 g	3 tbsp. (45 mL) cocoa powder plus 1 tbsp. (15 mL) butter
Chocolate (semisweet)	1 oz./30 g	as above + 1 tbsp. (15 mL) sugar
Cilantro	1 tbsp./15 mL	1 tbsp. (15 mL) parsley (flavor cannot be duplicated, for color only)
Cornstarch	1 tbsp./15 mL	2 tbsp. (30 mL) all-purpose flour
Flour, cake	1 cup/250 mL	1 cup (250 mL) all-purpose flour minus 2 tbsp. (30 mL)
Flour, self-rising	1 cup/250 mL	1 cup (250 mL) all-purpose flour plus $1^1/2$ tsp. (7 mL) baking powder plus $1/2$ tsp. (2 mL) salt
Herbs (fresh)	1 tbsp./15 mL	1 tsp. (5 mL) dried
Lemon zest (grated)	1 tsp./5 mL	1 tsp. (5 mL) lemon extract
Lemongrass (chopped)	1 stalk	1 tsp. (5 mL) grated lemon zest
Milk (sour)	1 cup/250 mL	1 cup (250 mL) minus 1 tbsp. (15 mL) then add 1 tbsp. (15 mL) vinegar OR lemon juice. Let stand 5 minutes; stir.
Milk (sweetened, condensed)	$10^1/2$ oz. (300 mL) can	Combine, in a blender, 1 cup + 2 tbsp. (280 mL) dry skim milk powder; 6 tbsp. (90 mL) boiling water; $3/4$ cup (175 mL) sugar; 3 tbsp. (45 mL) melted butter, 1 tsp. (5 mL) vanilla and a pinch of salt. Blend until very smooth. Refrigerate until cool. It thickens and makes $1^1/4$ cups (300 mL) or the equivalent of 1 can.

ITEM	QUANTITY	SUBSTITUTION
Mustard, prepared	1 tbsp./15 mL	1 tsp. (5 mL) dry or powdered mustard
Pine Nuts		blanched, slivered almonds
Romano Cheese	1/2 cup/125 mL	1/2 cup (125 mL) Parmesan cheese
Shallots	1/2 cup/125 mL	1/2 cup (125 mL) finely chopped onion plus 1/2 finely chopped garlic clove
Wine, Red	1 cup/250 mL	1 cup (250 mL) beef broth (not for desserts – for desserts try cranberry juice)
Wine, White	1 cup/250 mL	1 cup (250 mL) chicken broth (not for desserts – for desserts try white grape juice)
Beer	1 cup/250 mL	1 cup (250 mL) chicken OR beef broth
Yogurt (plain)	1 cup/250 mL	1 cup (250 mL) buttermilk

COOKING HELP & HINTS

- **Measuring Dry Ingredients**: When measuring flour and granulated or brown sugars for baking, use dry measuring cups and do the following: spoon the flour or granulated sugar into a dry measuring cup until heaping full. Level off the top evenly with a knife without shaking or tapping the ingredients. For brown sugar – pack the sugar firmly but lightly into the dry measuring cup and level the top.

- **Creaming Butter**: This is a very important step. Almost all baking recipes say "cream the butter and sugar until light and fluffy." Creaming incorporates tiny air bubbles into the butter – the more you cream, the lighter, fluffier and paler the mixture becomes. A cake that isn't creamed properly will be dense and heavy instead of light and airy. So, take that extra minute – the results will be worth it!

- **Toasting Nuts and Coconut**: Preheat the oven to 350°F (180°C). Spread the chopped nuts or coconut on a baking sheet or in a shallow pan and place in the preheated oven. Turn and mix occasionally until they are evenly toasted and golden or lightly browned, about 7–15 minutes depending on what you are toasting. Prepare a lot, cool and freeze for later use. Watch carefully so they don't burn.

SHARE THE
AISLES *of* ADVENTURE™
COOKBOOKS WITH A FRIEND

Please send:

_____ copies of *Discover Bananas* – $8.99

_____ copies of *Discover Strawberries* – $8.99

_____ Plus $4.00 (total order) for postage and handling

_____ Subtotal

_____ Add G.S.T. (subtotal X 7%) Canada only

_____ Total enclosed

U.S. and international orders $7.99, payable in U.S. Funds
Price is subject to change.

Name: _____

Address: _____

City: _____

Prov./State: _____   Postal/Zip Code: _____

Telephone: _____

Please make check or money order payable to:
Aisles of Adventure™
c/o HAK Publishing Inc.
#300, 8120 Beddington Blvd., NW
Calgary, Alberta, Canada T3K 2A8

Please allow 2-3 weeks for delivery.

www.aislesofadventure.com